Science in a Flash

Earth and Space

Georgia
Amson-Bradshaw

W
FRANKLIN WATTS
LONDON·SYDNEY

Franklin Watts
First published in Great Britain in 2017 by The Watts Publishing Group

Copyright © The Watts Publishing Group 2017

Produced for Franklin Watts by
White-Thomson Publishing Ltd
www.wtpub.co.uk

Credits
Series Editor: Georgia Amson-Bradshaw
Series Designer: Rocket Design (East Anglia) Ltd

Images from Shutterstock.com: Denis Shitikoff 5t, nickmoz 5c, Sarawut Padungkwan 5br, Michele Paccione 5br, silver tiger 6c, vectortatu 7tr, Yuriy Mazur 7c, Macrovector 8, Mopic 11c, Johan Swanepoel 13c, Designua 15t, Cristian Cestaro 16b, Fenton one 16bl, BlueRingMedia 17c, alessen 20t, angelinast 21c, Golden Sikorka 23, Vadim Sadovski 26bl, Vadim Sadovski 26c, 3Dsculptor 27l
Illustrations from other sources:
ATSZ56 wikicommons 15br, Soerfm wikicommons 24c, NASA 27r
Illustrations by Steve Evans: 4br, 4bl, 8c, 9br, 10br, 13b, 14c, 15bl, 18b, 19, 24bl, 24br
All design elements from Shutterstock.

Every attempt has been made to clear copyright.
Should there be any inadvertent omission
please apply to the publisher for rectification.

HB ISBN 978 1 4451 5274 5
PB ISBN 978 1 4451 5275 2

Printed in China

MIX
Paper from
responsible sources
FSC® C104740
FSC
www.fsc.org

Franklin Watts
An imprint of
Hachette Children's Group
Part of The Watts Publishing Group
Carmelite House
50 Victoria Embankment
London EC4Y 0DZ

An Hachette UK Company
www.hachette.co.uk

www.franklinwatts.co.uk

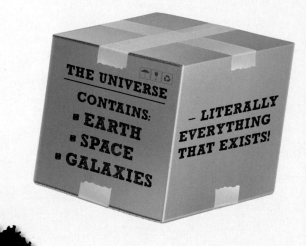

THE UNIVERSE CONTAINS:
■ EARTH
■ SPACE
■ GALAXIES
– LITERALLY EVERYTHING THAT EXISTS!

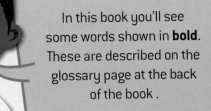

In this book you'll see some words shown in **bold**. These are described on the glossary page at the back of the book.

Contents

WHAT IS SPACE?

Look up at the sky on a clear night, and you will see a big black expanse filled with pinpricks of twinkling light. You are looking into space.

The universal truth

Earth's **atmosphere** ends about 100 kilometres from Earth's surface, and beyond that is space and the rest of the **Universe**. The Universe is what we call everything that exists – including Earth, space, and all the other planets, **stars** and **galaxies** within it.

THE UNIVERSE CONTAINS:
- EARTH
- SPACE
- GALAXIES

– LITERALLY EVERYTHING THAT EXISTS!

Space – it's in the name

Most of the Universe is made of empty space, a **vacuum** with no air. But dotted throughout are clumps of **matter** in the form of stars and planets.

Er, not that type of vacuum ...

Did you know?

Humans can't survive for more than about 90 seconds if accidentally exposed to the vacuum of space. That's why astronauts wear pressurised space suits when outside their space crafts.

How big?

The Universe is very, very big. The distances are difficult to wrap your head round! If the Sun was the size of a basketball, Earth would be the size of a pea, 28 metres away (a few metres longer than a tennis court). The next nearest star to our sun would be another basketball 9,000 kilometres away!

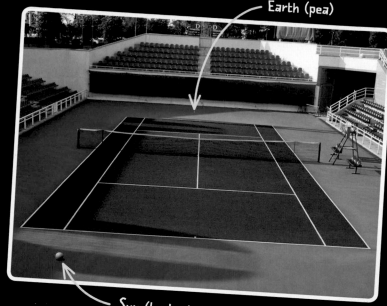

Earth (pea)

Sun (basketball)

Galaxies in space are still moving apart.

The Big Bang

Most scientists believe that the Universe began 13.8 billion years ago with an event called the Big Bang. They think that the entire Universe was squashed into an unimaginably tiny, dense ball, which exploded outwards in a fraction of a second. We can see from the movements of stars and galaxies that the Universe is still expanding outwards today.

FACT ATTACK

Size and Shape

If 13.8 billion years of our Universe were condensed into a single year, Earth would form in mid-September, the dinosaurs would appear on the 25th of December (Christmas Day), and humans would exist for just the last 20 seconds of the entire year.

Merry Christmas!

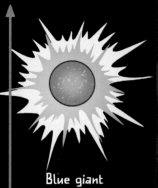

Blue giant

White star

Yellow star

Orange star

Red dwarf star

COOLEST (although they're all pretty hot!)

All about stars and galaxies

Stars are giant balls of burning gas.
Galaxies are big groups of stars.

Most of the twinkling lights that you can see in the night sky are stars. Others are planets and galaxies. Galaxies are huge groups of stars, dust and gas.

Our star

The Sun is a star, the closest one to us. Stars are big balls of burning gas, held together by **gravity**, that give out light and heat.

Cool colours

To the naked eye, stars look like small white dots. But powerful **telescopes** show there is a big variety of sizes, temperatures and colours. These different types of stars have names. A red dwarf is a small red star. A blue giant is a large blue star. The colours tell you how hot a star is: red is the coolest, increasing in heat through orange, yellow, white to blue, the hottest.

Life of a star

Stars begin as a big, swirling, colourful cloud of gas, called a **nebula**. Stars die when they run out of fuel, but they don't fade out like a candle or a fire on Earth. They end in a huge explosion called a **supernova**.

Galaxy gazing

Most stars in the Universe are part of galaxies. A single galaxy can contain anything from several million to over a trillion stars, and they range in size from a few thousand to several hundred thousand **light years** across. Galaxies come in different shapes, including spiral, elliptical (or egg-shaped) and irregular.

Spilt milk

Our galaxy is called the **Milky Way**, and it is a spiral galaxy. It contains 200 billion stars, and is 100,000 light years across. The Milky Way gets its name because from Earth it looks like a milky white splash across the sky. The ancient Greeks called it 'galaxias kyklos', or 'milky circle', and the Romans called it 'via lactea', or 'road of milk'.

Two galaxies colliding

FACT ATTACK

Galaxies

There are over one billion galaxies in the Universe, and like stars they can be found alone, in pairs or in groups called clusters.

What is THE SOLAR SYSTEM?

The solar system is our sun and all the things that go around it.

At the centre of our **solar system** is a star that we call the Sun. There are eight planets, including Earth, that move in a circle around the Sun. As well as these eight planets there are **asteroids, comets** and moons.

My very educated mother ...

The eight planets that make up our solar system are Mercury, Venus, Earth, Mars, Jupiter, Saturn, Uranus and Neptune. You can remember this order by thinking of this silly sentence: My Very Educated Mother Just Served Us Noodles. Can you think of your own silly sentence?

Mars

Earth

Venus

Mercury

Oval orbit

Each of these planets **orbits** the Sun, which means they spin in an oval shape around it. The force that holds the solar system together and keeps these planets and their moons orbiting the Sun is gravity. The planets don't all move at the same speed around the Sun. Instead, those planets closest to the Sun move faster, while the ones further away orbit more slowly.

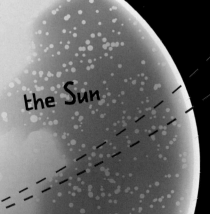

the Sun

Poor little Pluto

Until 2006, scientists thought there was a ninth planet called Pluto. But they now think Pluto is too small to be a proper planet, and is instead a **dwarf planet**.

Neptune

Uranus

Saturn

Jupiter

Sorry Pluto, you're not a planet after all.

Give it a go!

The picture on this page makes it seem like the planets are all quite close together. In fact, the distances between them are huge! Make a scale model of the first four planets to get an idea of how big our solar system really is.

You will need four friends, a big outdoor space such as a football field, a metre rule or wheel, a football, two peppercorns and two peas.

Have the first person hold the football and stand at the edge of your open space. They are the Sun.

Have the second person hold a peppercorn. Measuring with the metre rule or wheel, have them walk 12 metres away from the Sun. They are Mercury.

Venus needs a pea, and should walk 21 metres away from the Sun. Earth also holds a pea, and walks 28 metres from the Sun. Mars holds a peppercorn, and walks 45 metres away.

To include Neptune, someone would need to stand nearly one kilometre away!

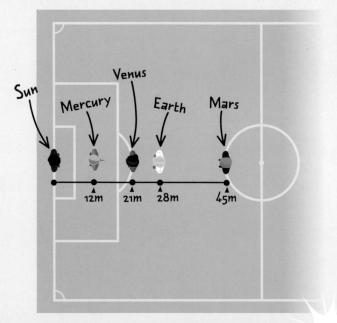

All about the SUN

The Sun is a star.
Earth spins around the Sun.

Although it looks very different to the stars that you see at night, the Sun is a star too. Our sun is a yellow dwarf star, so it's a small, cool star compared to others in the Universe. Like all stars, it is a huge burning ball made mostly of two gases, hydrogen and helium, held together by gravity.

Who are you calling a dwarf?

Although it's small compared to other stars, the Sun is huge compared to Earth. At around 1,392,000 kilometres in diameter, it is about 110 times the diameter of Earth.

Woah! This tiny speck is Earth, drawn to the same scale as the Sun on this page.

sunspots

Not too hot, not too cold ...

Did you know?

Liquid water can exist on Earth because of our distance from the Sun. If we were further away, it would be too cold and all water would freeze. If we were closer, the water would boil away. This area of space is nicknamed the 'Goldilocks zone'.

Hot at heart

The Sun is not the same temperature all the way through. The core, right in the middle, is the hottest part, at 15 million degrees Celsius! The surface of the Sun is around 5,500 degrees Celsius, but there are darker areas on the Sun's surface which are cooler. These are called sunspots, and they can be viewed from Earth if you look through a solar filter – but you should NEVER look directly at the Sun.

surface

core

Solar telescope with filter

Light of life

The Sun provides all the heat and light that we get on Earth, and is essential for all life on our planet. Without the Sun, Earth's surface temperature would be around -270 degrees Celsius. Brrrr!

Riddle me this!

Why do you think the Sun is so important to sustaining life on planet Earth? Here's a clue:

Answer on page 28.

All about EARTH

Our home planet is unique in the solar system. It is a rocky **sphere** or ball covered mostly by water, surrounded by an atmosphere that contains **oxygen**. With each of these ingredients, it can support life.

Grown by gravity

Like all planets, Earth was created by gravity. Dust and gas swirling around in space were slowly pulled together by gravity into the rocky ball that exists now.

Fresh air

Just as important as the solid rock that we stand on, is the gassy layer around Earth that is our atmosphere. It contains oxygen that we need to breathe, and acts like a protective blanket, keeping Earth's surface at a fairly stable temperature.

12

Inside Earth

If you were able to cut Earth in half down the middle, you would see that it has several layers.

The top layer is called the **crust**, which is made of huge rocky plates, as thick as 75 km in some places, but as thin as 5 km in others.

Below the crust is the **mantle**, a semi-solid layer of very hot rock.

The next layer down is the **outer core,** which is made of the liquid metals iron and nickel.

At the centre is the **inner core**, which is solid iron and nickel.

The atmosphere is the gas layer around the outside. We see it during the day as the blue sky.

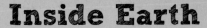

Give it a go!

Ever wondered why is the sky blue during the day, but at sunset is reddish-orange? This experiment recreates the effect of sunlight in our atmosphere. You'll need a transparent plastic box filled with water, some milk or milk powder, and a torch.

Place the torch so the beam shines through the middle of the water-filled box. Add milk or milk powder to the water until you can see the beam of light clearly.

Look at the beam of light from the side of the box. It should appear blue-ish white in colour. Now look at the beam from the end. It should look yellowish orange. What do you think is going on here? **Find out on page 28!**

Viewed from the side the light looks blue-ish white.

torch

Viewed from the end the light looks yellowish orange.

How does Earth move?

Earth spins on its axis and orbits around the Sun.

Although Earth feels completely still to us, in fact it is spinning around on its point, or its **axis**, like a basketball spinning on someone's finger. It takes 24 hours for Earth to turn around once on its axis, and it is this spinning of Earth that gives us night and day.

Sunrise, sunset

Sit on a swivel chair, keeping your head facing forward at all times. Have a friend stand in front of you, holding a ball. Now spin on the chair (keeping your head straight). See how the ball moves across your field of vision from one side to the other, until it passes out of sight behind you.

This is the same way that the Sun appears to rise and set in the sky. When we are facing away from the Sun, we have night-time. When we are facing towards the Sun, we have daytime.

POP QUIZ!

How long does Earth take to turn once on its axis?
a) **One whole day**
b) **One month**
c) **One year**
Answer on page 28.

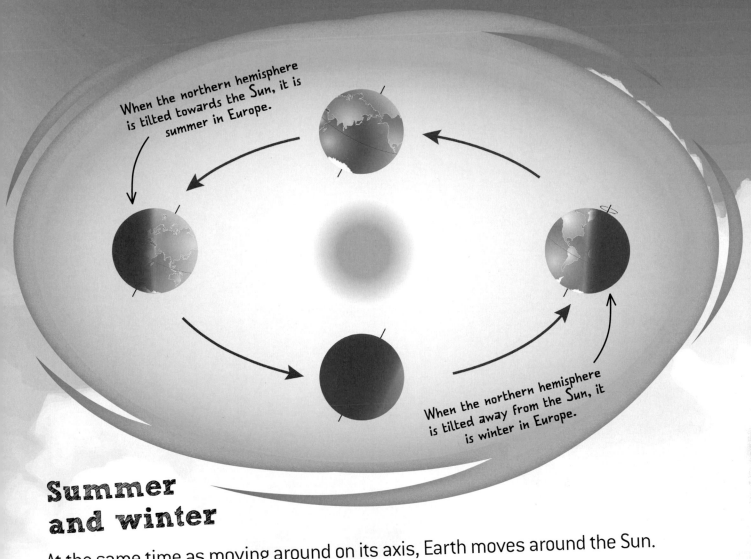

When the northern hemisphere is tilted towards the Sun, it is summer in Europe.

When the northern hemisphere is tilted away from the Sun, it is winter in Europe.

Summer and winter

At the same time as moving around on its axis, Earth moves around the Sun. It takes 365 days (one year) to complete one full orbit. Because Earth is slightly tilted, and the tilt of Earth does not change, parts of Earth are closer to the Sun at certain times of year. This is what gives us the seasons.

Did you know?

The Sun was very important to many ancient peoples. The Maya built stone temples that aligned with the Sun's position on important days of the year. A temple at Chichen Itza in Mexico is built so that on the **spring equinox**, the Sun casts a shadow in the shape of a snake wriggling down the side of the pyramid!

How does the Moon move?

The Moon orbits Earth and spins slowly on its axis.

The Moon goes round Earth once roughly every 28 days. This is called the **lunar month**. The word 'month' comes from 'moon-th'!

The changing Moon

Over a month, the Moon appears to shrink to a crescent before disappearing totally, then grows again into a full circle.

In fact, one side of the Moon is fully lit up by the Sun at all times, but it isn't always the side facing Earth. We see just a part of the lit side, making it appear to be a different shape. The changes in the appearance of the Moon are called the **phases of the Moon**.

The Sun always lights up one side of the Moon.

the Sun

The Moon orbits the Earth.

Viewed from Earth, this is what the phases look like.

The Moon looks thin and pale. Is she OK?

Don't worry, it's just a phase.

An **orrery** is a model of the solar system, showing how the planets and moons move around the Sun. Make a simple paper orrery of the Sun, Earth, and the Moon.

You'll need a big piece of paper or card, scissors, two split pin paper fasteners, a compass, and colouring pencils.

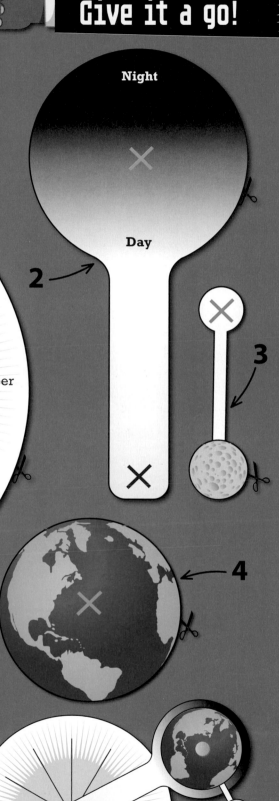

1

January
February
December
March
November
April
October
May
September
June
August
July

Night

2

Day

3

4

Copy shapes 1 to 4, including the markings, onto a large piece of paper or card, and cut them out. Poke holes in the pieces using a pencil where the red and blue crosses are.

Now fix your pieces together using the fasteners. Match the red crosses using the first fastener, to join piece 1 with the stem of piece 2. Match the blue crosses using the second fastener to join pieces 2, 3, and 4.

Your finished orrery should look like this:

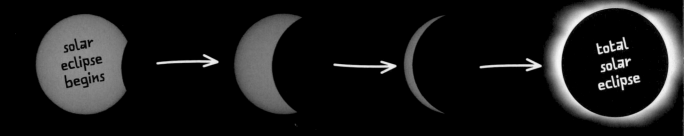

WHAT IS AN ECLIPSE?

An eclipse is when the Sun or Moon are hidden from view because of their position in space.

There are two types of eclipse that we can see on Earth. One is a **solar eclipse**, where the Sun is blocked from view by the Moon. The other is a **lunar eclipse**, where Earth blocks the Sun's light and casts a dark shadow on the Moon.

Blackout

During a solar eclipse, a black disc starts to slowly move across the surface of the Sun. This is the Moon moving into a straight line between the Sun and Earth, and casting a shadow. When the Moon is directly in line between the Sun and Earth, from a certain point on Earth, only a ring of bright light can be seen around the Moon's edge.

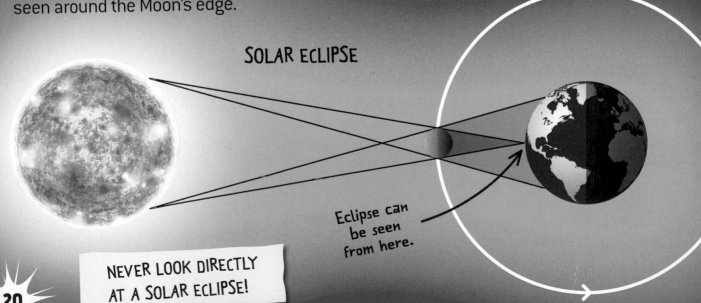

SOLAR ECLIPSE

Eclipse can be seen from here.

NEVER LOOK DIRECTLY AT A SOLAR ECLIPSE!

20

solar eclipse ends

Hey!

Partial eclipse

Not all eclipses are 'total' eclipses where the whole Sun or Moon are covered. In fact, during a solar eclipse, the Sun will only appear totally blocked from a small area on Earth. Other places will see a 'partial' eclipse, where some of the Sun remains visible, like a bite has been taken out of it!

Earth shadow

Lunar eclipses can only happen at full moon. They occur when Earth moves between the Sun and the Moon, blocking the Sun's light. Because we can only see the Moon through the reflected light of the Sun, blocking the Sun's light causes the Moon to darken or 'disappear'.

LUNAR ECLIPSE

FACT ATTACK

There are between two and five lunar eclipses a year.

Did you know?

The Moon doesn't completely disappear during a lunar eclipse, it is normally still at least slightly visible. This is because Earth's atmosphere bends a small amount of the Sun's light, which still falls on the Moon. As red light is best able to travel through Earth's atmosphere, the Moon often ends up bathed in an eerie, blood-red glow ...

21

All about the PLANETS

There are three other rocky planets and four gas planets in our solar system.

Mercury, Venus and Mars are made of rock, like Earth. Jupiter, Saturn, Uranus and Neptune are huge balls of gas with only a small rocky core at the centre. They are called the 'gas giants'.

Mars

gets much colder than Earth. But evidence of water on Mars has scientists wondering if tiny alien organisms, similar to bacteria, have ever lived on the planet!

Venus

is Earth's closest neighbour, but it isn't much like Earth. The atmosphere is thick and poisonous, and the pressure is so great you would be instantly crushed to death.

Mercury

is the closest planet to the Sun. It has a very thin atmosphere, so the surface can heat up to 450 degrees Celsius during the day, and drop to -183 degrees Celsius at night.

Which planet do you think has the shortest year?

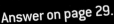
Answer on page 29.

Jupiter

is the largest planet in our solar system, and it has the most moons. It is a gas giant, meaning if you parachuted onto it, you'd never find a firm landing site!

Saturn

is the second largest planet and is surrounded by bands of rings made of rock, dust and ice. It has 62 moons, and can be seen in the night sky without a telescope.

Uranus

is unusual because rather than spinning with its poles at the top and bottom, it spins on its side. Being so far from the Sun, one year on Uranus lasts 84 Earth years. Uranus and Neptune are called Ice Giants, as they are made of frozen gases.

Neptune

takes 164 Earth years to orbit once round the Sun. It has cold winds that blow over 2,000 km/h.

Asteroids, comets and meteors

Lumps of rock and ice move through space, and sometimes hit planets and moons

Planets and their moons aren't the only objects that orbit the Sun. There is a lot of dust, rock and icy chunks of frozen gas that are left over from when the planets first formed. These are asteroids and comets.

Space snowballs

Comets are giant lumps of frozen gases and dust, and when they pass close to the Sun, the frozen gases turn into vapour, leaving a tail of gas and dust behind them.

Space rocks

Asteroids are made of just rock, not ice. Most asteroids in our solar system can be found in the asteroid belt, a rocky ring about 300–500 million kilometres from the Sun. Some asteroids are hundreds of kilometres across, while others are as small as one metre.

Shooting stars

When a small bit of rock or ice enters Earth's atmosphere, it burns up creating a streak of light. These are called **meteors**, or shooting stars. Many people believe seeing a meteor is good luck. If the piece of rock is big enough to reach the ground without burning up completely, we call it a **meteorite**.

Fatal impact

When a meteorite hits a planet, the force of impact can create a big hole called a crater. If the meteorite is very big, it can cause huge amounts of dust to be thrown up into the atmosphere, which then has a cooling effect on the climate. Scientists believe the dust from a meteorite hitting Earth was the final blow that killed off the dinosaurs.

Oh, a shooting star! That's good luck!

Give it a go!

See how meteorites form craters on Earth. You'll need a large tray, a bag of flour, some cocoa powder, a sieve and some 'meteorites' such as marbles of different sizes, or rubber balls.

Fill the tray with flour a few centimetres deep, then with a sieve add a thin layer of the cocoa powder on top. This will help you see how the dust is thrown up by your meteorite impacts.

Throw or drop your mini-meteorites from different distances into the tray. How big are the craters that are formed? What does the pattern of flour and cocoa powder around your craters look like?

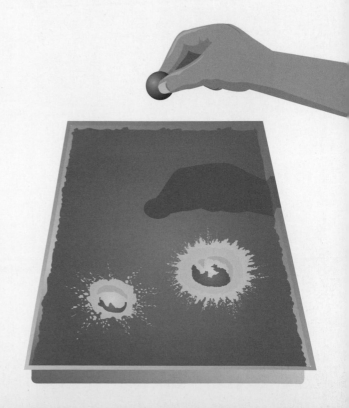

ALL ABOUT
SPACE EXPLORATION

Humans and robots are exploring space right now.

People have been fascinated by space throughout history. We are constantly developing technologies to help us better understand the Universe beyond our planet's atmosphere.

Seeing stars

In the 17th century, the famous astronomer Galileo revolutionised people's understanding of our solar system by observing the stars and planets with one of the earliest telescopes. Since then we have been creating more and more powerful telescopes to learn about our Universe. Modern telescopes in orbit around Earth can detect light coming from billions of light years away.

an astronaut

The new James Webb Space Telescope is designed with a large mirror sitting on top of a sun-shield. The powerful telescope can detect heat from new stars.

To boldly go

As well as looking at the Universe, we have been visiting it. The first person in space was Russian astronaut Yuri Gagarin, who orbited Earth once in a 108-minute flight in 1961. Since 2000, the International Space Station has had astronauts permanently living on board, conducting scientific research.

The International Space Station

NASA's robot rover Curiosity

Rocket science

Leaving the pull of Earth's gravity takes massive amounts of energy and fuel – a space craft has to travel at 40,000 km/h to get into space! Once in space, the distances are massive, and travelling even to the nearest planets Venus and Mars takes months. But where humans cannot yet go, robots are already exploring. NASA's robot rover Curiosity is investigating the surface of Mars right now.

A space craft has to travel at 40,000 kilometres per hour to get into space!

POP QUIZ!

Where do you think it is better to position a powerful telescope:
a) at sea level
b) on a mountain
c) in space
Answer on page 29.

And the answer is ...

Page 11

Riddle me this: Without the Sun, all our water and food sources would not exist. It would be so cold that all water would be frozen. Plants which get their energy directly from the Sun would all die, so all animals and humans that eat plants would run out of food too. Without plants, we would also have no oxygen to breathe.

Page 13

Give it a go: The Sun gives out white light, which contains all the different colours of light. When sunlight hits Earth's atmosphere, some of the light is 'scattered' or bounced around in the air. Blue light is most easily scattered, so the blue light bouncing around in the air makes the sky look blue. At sunset, because of the angle the Sun is at, light has to travel through much more of the atmosphere before it reaches your eyes than when the Sun is directly overhead. By the time the light has travelled through so much atmosphere, the blue light has been scattered out in the distance and the only light that reaches you is reddish-orange.

Page 14

Pop quiz: The answer is a), Earth takes one whole day to turn around on its axis.

Page 17

Riddle me this: Without an atmosphere, there is no wind on the Moon. So astronauts' footprints can last for years, as they don't get blown away.

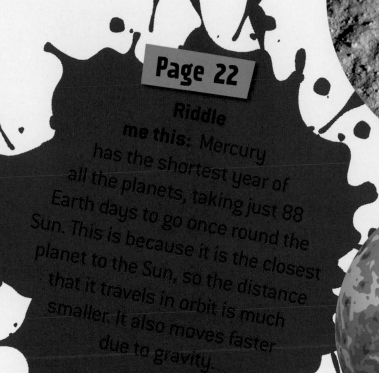

Page 22

Riddle me this: Mercury has the shortest year of all the planets, taking just 88 Earth days to go once round the Sun. This is because it is the closest planet to the Sun, so the distance that it travels in orbit is much smaller. It also moves faster due to gravity.

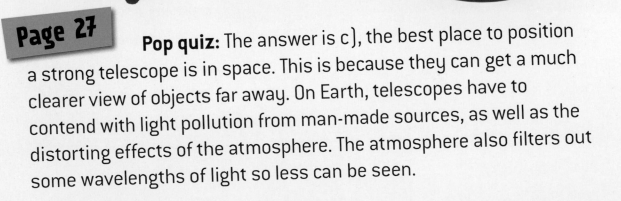

Page 27

Pop quiz: The answer is c), the best place to position a strong telescope is in space. This is because they can get a much clearer view of objects far away. On Earth, telescopes have to contend with light pollution from man-made sources, as well as the distorting effects of the atmosphere. The atmosphere also filters out some wavelengths of light so less can be seen.

Glossary

Asteroid A piece of rock that orbits the Sun

Atmosphere
The blanket of gases that surround some planets, including Earth

Axis The imaginary line that runs down through the middle of Earth from the North Pole to the South Pole

Comet A chunk of ice, dust and rock that moves through space. When near the Sun, they develop tails of gas and dust

Crater A hole on the surface of a planet or moon caused by a rock hitting it

Crust The outer rocky layer of Earth

Dwarf planet A spherical object that orbits the Sun, but that isn't big enough to be classified a full planet

Galaxy A huge group of stars held together by gravity

Gravity A pulling force that exists between two objects in space. Larger objects have a stronger gravitational pull

Inner core The layer right at the centre of Earth made of solid metal

Light year A measure of distance in space: how far light travels in one year

Mantle Earth's middle layer, made of semi-solid rock

Matter All physical 'stuff' in the Universe

Meteor A small piece of rock that enters Earth's atmosphere and burns up in a streak of light

Meteorite A piece of rock big enough to enter Earth's atmosphere and reach the ground without burning up entirely

Milky Way The name for the galaxy that contains our solar system

Nebula A cloud of dust and gas where new stars can form

Orbit To travel around a body in space

Orrery A mechanical model of the solar system

Outer core The layer near the centre of our Earth made of molten metal

Oxygen The gas in our atmosphere that we need to breathe

Phases of the Moon
The different amount of the Moon that is visible each night across the month

Satellite A natural or man-made object that orbits another body in space

Solar system A sun and the planets and other bodies that orbit it

Sphere A ball shape

Spring equinox The day of the year in Spring when the day and night are the same length

Star A huge ball of burning gases held together by gravity

Supernova The explosion of a star at the end of its life

Telescope A device for looking at distant objects

Universe Earth, space and everything that exists

Vacuum A space that contains nothing at all, not even air

Further reading

Straight Forward with Science:
Earth in Space
Peter Riley (Franklin Watts, 2015)

Watch This Space!:
Astronomy, Astronauts and Space Exploration
Clive Gifford (Wayland, 2016)

The Real Scientist:
Space! Our Solar System and Beyond
Peter Riley (Franklin Watts, 2012)

The Story of Space: Space Stations
Steve Parker (Franklin Watts, 2015)

Space Travel Guides: The Outer Planets
Giles Sparrow (Franklin Watts, 2013)

Websites

joshworth.com/dev/pixelspace/pixelspace_solarsystem.html
Scale model of the solar system online: great fun to play with!

www.bbc.co.uk/education/topics/zkbbkqt
Video clips all about Earth and space

www.nasa.gov/kidsclub
Information, pictures and more from NASA, especially for kids

www.esa.int/esaKIDSen/
Fun games, projects and more from the European Space Agency

Every effort has been made by the Publishers to ensure that the websites in this book are suitable for children, that they are of the highest educational value, and that they contain no inappropriate or offensive material. However, because of the nature of the Internet, it is impossible to guarantee that the contents of these sites will not be altered. We strongly advise that Internet access is supervised by a responsible adult.

Index

Science in a Flash
Series contents lists

Earth and Space

• What is space? • All about stars and galaxies • What is the solar system? • All about the Sun • All about the Earth • How does the Earth move? • All about the Moon • How does the Moon move? • What is an eclipse? • All about the planets • What are asteroids and comets? • All about space travel

Living things

• What is a living thing? • How are living things grouped? • What is a habitat? • All about food chains • Producers, predators and prey • The life cycle of a mammal • The life cycle of an amphibian • The life cycle of an insect • The life cycle of a bird • All about reproduction • What is evolution? • Our changing environment

Electricity

• What is electricity? • Where does electricity come from? • What do we use electricity for? • All about static electricity • Electrical current and circuits • Conductors and insulators • All about batteries • Electricity and magnetism • How do we make electricity? • All about renewable energy • How do we measure electricity? • Powering circuits

Rocks

• What are Rocks? • All about our rocky planet • What are igneous rocks? • What are sedimentary rocks? • What are metamorphic rocks? • All about the rock cycle • All about erosion and weathering • What are the properties of rocks? • All about fossils • All about soil • What are precious stones? • Amazing rocks

Forces

• What is a force? • Forces around us • What is gravity? • What is magnetism? • All about friction • What is air resistance? • What is water resistance? • All about upthrust • All about elasticity • Balanced and unbalanced forces • All about pressure • Making forces bigger

Sound

• What is sound? • Sound on the move • Loud and soft • Sound and hearing • What is an echo? • Blocking sound • Ultrasound and infrasound • Animal hearing • What is music? • Recording sounds • Sound and science

Light

• What is light? • Sources of light • Light on the move • Light and materials • What are shadows? • What is reflection? • What is refraction? • Colourful light • Light and sight • Light and life • Types of light • Light and health

States of Matter

• Materials and matter • States of matter • All about solids • All about liquids • All about gases • Melting and freezing • Evaporating, boiling and condensing • The water cycle • What is a mixture? • Separating mixtures • Permanent state changes • The future of materials